CAIRN TERRIER OWNERS GUIDE

The Best Guide On The Care, Raising, Feeding, Socializing, Breeding, Exercise, Health, Cost, Complete Management And Loving Your Dog

DR. OKUS OSCAR

Table of Contents

CHAPTER ONE 4
  Cairn Terrier 4
  Is It All Worthwhile In The End? 6
  How Healthy Is Your Cairn Terrier? 8

CHAPTER THREE 13
  Information Regarding The General Health Of Your Cairn Terrier 13
  Diseases Of The Teeth 13
  Infections 14
  Obesity 15
  Parasites 16
  Castration Or Sterilization (S/N) 18

CHAPTER FOUR 21
  Problems With The Liver Can Be Genetically Predisposed In Cairn Terriers 21
  Eye Problems 23
  Diabetes 27
  Knee Problems 29

CHAPTER FIVE 31
  A Lack Of Pyruvate Kinase In The Body 31
  Bleeding Disorders 32

Allergies 35

Liver Problems 36

CHAPTER SIX 40

Cushing's Syndrome Is Also Known As Hyperadrenocorticism 40

Necrosis Of The Hip 41

Coronary Artery Disease 42

Bladder Or Kidney Stones 45

Dysplasia Of The Hip And Elbow 46

Disorders Of The Kidneys 47

CHAPTER SEVEN 49

How To Take Care Of Your Cairn Terrier When You're Not At Home 49

Care Routines, Diet, And Physical Activity ...51

What To Keep An Eye Out For 54

THE END 56

CHAPTER ONE

Cairn Terrier

Your dog is one of a kind! She is your most trusted confidante, constant companion, and a wellspring of affection that is never conditional. There is a good chance that you picked her because you like Cairns and you anticipated that she would have specific characteristics that would be compatible with your way of life:

- Vibrant, having a warm and welcoming personality

- Enjoys playing games, especially fetch

- Is a devoted friend and member of the family dog breed

- Its coat is short and easy to care for; it's easily motivated and trainable; it's small but sturdy; and it has a low maintenance coat.

On the other hand, no dog is perfect. It's possible that you've also observed the following characteristics:

- Must have a lot of physical and mental stimulation in order to prevent boredom from leading to vices.

- Brave and fearless, and therefore capable of attacking much larger dogs

- Likely to attack other small animals, especially cats

- Likely to attack larger dogs

- Easily distracted and prone to getting into trouble

- Enjoys digging

- If you can't demonstrate strong leadership, they can be willful and stubborn.

Is It All Worthwhile In The End?

Of course! She has a lot of character, which is one of the

reasons you like her so much. The Cairn Terrier is a friend that is both fast to learn and full of enthusiasm. She adores entertaining audiences with magic acts and interacting with young children.

The Cairn Terrier was first produced in Scotland over 200 years ago with the purpose of reducing the number of rodents living in rock piles. Its origins may be traced back to Scotland. The Cairn adores spending time with children and is a quick study when it comes to picking up new skills. The role of "Toto" in "The Wizard of Oz" was played by a Cairn

Terrier, which led to the increased popularity of the breed as a pet. The Cairn Terrier is a tough breed that typically lives between 13 and 14 years on average. As is the case with many breeds, they are prone to certain health problems, including as diabetes and patellar luxation, which must be monitored closely. Be sure to schedule routine exams for yourself because early detection is the key to living a long and happy life.

How Healthy Is Your Cairn Terrier?

We are aware that you feel an immense amount of responsibility for your dog, and as a result, you want to provide the best possible care for her. Because of this, we have compiled a summary of the various health concerns that we intend to discuss with you for the duration of your Cairn. Because Cairn Terriers have their own set of unique health issues, we need to be aware of those issues in order to devise a strategy for avoiding potential dangers and hopefully avoiding them altogether.

There are a number of diseases and problems that are genetic, which means they are tied to the breed of your pet. The researchers who study canine genetics and the veterinarians who practice them have come to the conclusion that the diseases we've mentioned in this article have a considerable rate of occurrence and/or influence in this breed of dog. That does not mean that these issues will manifest themselves in your dog; rather, it indicates that she is at a greater risk than other dogs. In order to give you an idea of what may be in store for her in the future, we are going to detail the most prevalent health problems that are observed in Cairn Terriers. Naturally, we are unable to cover every possibilities in this article; thus, make sure to get in touch with us if you observe any peculiar indications or symptoms.

The most essential genetic predispositions for Cairn Terriers are discussed in this book, in addition to general health information that is relevant to canines in general and all other breeds. Having this information allows you and us to collaborate on a plan to meet the one-of-a-kind medical requirements of your pet. We have also included, towards the very end of the brochure, a summary of what you can do on a daily basis at home to ensure that your Cairn always looks and feels her very best. You will be aware of what to look out for, and the knowledge that we are providing your friend with the highest level of care will make all of us feel better.

CHAPTER THREE

Information Regarding The General Health Of Your Cairn Terrier

Diseases Of The Teeth

Dental disease is the most frequent form of chronic illness that can be seen in pets; by the age of two, it affects eighty percent of all dogs. And it's terrible, but your Cairn Terrier has a higher risk of developing dental issues compared to other types of dogs. The formation of tartar on the teeth is the initial step, followed by infection of the gums and the tooth roots as the condition worsens. Your friend will lose her teeth and be at risk of experiencing damage to her kidneys, liver, heart, and joints if we do not take measures to prevent or cure dental disease on her behalf. In point of fact, the lifespan of your Cairn Terrier may be shortened by anything from one to three years! We'll give your dog's teeth a professional cleaning on a regular basis and advise you on what you can do to maintain their gleaming whiteness at home.

Infections

Cairn Terriers are susceptible to bacterial and viral illnesses, including parvovirus, rabies, and distemper. These are the same kind of infections that can affect other breeds of dogs. We will prescribe vaccination for her since it is the best way to protect her against the diseases that are prevalent in our area, as well as her age and other considerations. Many of these infections are preventable.

Obesity

Obesity can be a severe health problem in Cairn Terriers. It is a dangerous condition that has the potential to cause or worsen back pain, metabolic and digestive difficulties, joint problems, and heart disease. Though it's tempting to offer your companion food when she looks at you with those adoring eyes, you can "love her to death" with leftover people food and doggie goodies. Instead, you should give her a cuddle, brush her fur or teeth, play a game with her, or maybe even take her on a walk. She'll appreciate it. You will feel better after she does, and so will she!

Parasites

Both the interior and the outside of your Cairn can be infested with many sorts of worms and vermin. Her skin and ears are susceptible to infestation from a wide variety of parasites, including fleas, ticks, and ear mites. It is possible for her body to become infected with hookworms, roundworms, heartworms, and whipworms through a variety of means, including ingesting contaminated water, walking barefoot on polluted soil, or being bitten by an infected mosquito. Some of these parasites have the potential to be passed on to you or a member of your family, making them a significant cause for concern for everyone. It is critical that we perform regular checks for the presence of these parasites because they can cause your canine companion pain, discomfort, and even death. Therefore, it is necessary that we perform these checks. In addition, we will offer recommendations for preventative medication that may be required to keep her healthy.

Castration Or Sterilization (S/N)

It is in your best interest to get your Cairn spayed, as this is one of the most beneficial things you can do for her (neutered for males). When performing this procedure on a female patient, the ovaries and the uterus are surgically removed. When performing this procedure on a male patient, the testicles are surgically removed.

The risk of developing some forms of cancer is reduced when a pet is spayed or neutered, and you no longer have to worry about your animal producing litters of pups or kittens that you don't want. While your pet is under anesthesia for this procedure, we will be able to diagnose and treat some of the ailments that your dog is likely to develop in the future. This offers us the opportunity to better care for your dog. For instance, if your pet requires hip X-rays or if a puppy tooth has to be pulled, now would be an excellent time to schedule such procedures. This is a simple solution for both you and your friend, which is convenient. Testing the patient's blood on a routine basis before to surgery enables us to recognize common issues that raise the risk of anesthesia or operation and to take appropriate preventative measures. Don't worry; when the time comes, we'll talk about the particular issues that we'll be looking for and how to spot them.

CHAPTER FOUR

Problems With The Liver Can Be Genetically Predisposed In Cairn Terriers

Your Cairn is more likely than other dogs to suffer from a condition known as portosystemic shunt, which affects the liver (PSS). Because a portion of the blood supply that ought to go to the liver instead flows around it, the liver is deprived of the blood flow that is necessary for it to develop and operate appropriately. In the event that your friend has PSS, his liver will be unable to properly eliminate poisons from his bloodstream. Every time he gets anesthesia, we will evaluate his liver function in addition to performing a routine pre-anesthetic panel so that we can make sure that he does not have this condition.

In the event that he develops symptoms like slowed growth or seizures, we will test his blood and perhaps perform an ultrasound check of his liver. It's possible that surgery will be required, but in certain instances, we can treat the condition with a specialized diet and some medications.

Eye Problems

There aren't many things that can have as significant of an effect on the quality of life of your dog as ensuring that his eyes are healthy and functioning properly.

Cairn Terriers can unfortunately inherit or develop a number of different eye conditions, some of which can cause blindness if they are not treated right away, and the majority of which can be extremely painful! Unfortunately, Cairn Terriers can inherit or develop a number of different eye conditions. At each exam, we will check his eyes to see if there are any warning signals that could cause worry.

Glaucoma is a disease that causes severe pain and, if ignored, can quickly lead to blindness in Cairn Terriers and humans alike. Glaucoma is an eye disorder that affects people as well as Cairn Terriers. Squinting, watery eyes, bluing of the cornea (the transparent front part of the eye), and redness in the whites of the eyes are some of the symptoms that come along with dry eye syndrome. Pain is frequently present, but owners of pets very seldom perceive it, despite the fact that it can be rather severe. People who experience specific varieties of glaucoma frequently describe the sensation as being similar to that of having an ice pick thrust into their eye. Yikes! In more severe cases, the eye may appear enlarged or swollen, giving the impression that it is bulging outward. We will conduct his annual glaucoma screening in order to diagnose him as soon as possible and get him started on therapy. Glaucoma is a condition that must be treated immediately. If you see any symptoms, don't hesitate to give us a call; instead, head to the nearest emergency room.

Cataracts are a leading cause of vision loss among people in their later years in Cairns. When we check him, we will be on the lookout for the lenses in his eyes to grow more opaque, which means that they will appear foggy rather than clear. Despite their eyesight loss, many dogs are able to adapt positively and have normal lives. There is also the possibility of undergoing surgery to have cataracts surgically removed and one's vision restored.

A disorder known as distichiasis is brought on when additional hairs grow on the inside of the eyelid and irritate the surface of the eye as they rub against it. Your Cairn has a higher risk than other dogs do of developing this excruciating condition, which is one of the diseases that is passed down in dogs the most frequently. These aberrant hairs, if left untreated, can lead to ulcers in the cornea as well as chronic eye pain. There are a number of therapeutic methods available, and the prognosis is favorable after the hairs have been removed in a way that is irreversible.

Diabetes

The condition known as diabetes mellitus affects a significant number of dogs. It is possible for any breed to be affected, although Cairns have a higher prevalence than usual. Diabetic dogs are unable to control the amount of sugars that are metabolized in their bodies and require insulin injections on a daily basis. Because of the severity of the ailment, it is essential to get a diagnosis and begin treatment as soon as practicable. In addition to a reduction in body mass, symptoms include an increase in the frequency of urinating, drinking, and eating. We will do lab testing to identify if he has this condition and discuss treatment options with you if he exhibits signs of having it. If he does, we will treat him. The treatment calls for a significant investment of both one's time and one's resources. Today, diabetic dogs who are well controlled by their owners have the same life expectancy as normal canines.

Knee Problems

It's possible that the patella, or kneecap, of your Cairn will move about occasionally (called patellar luxation). It's possible that you'll observe that as he runs along, he occasionally kicks up one foot behind him and skips or hops for a few steps. Then, he pops his kneecap back into position by kicking his leg out to the side, and everything is normal after that. If the issue is not severe and affects only one leg, your friend may not need much treatment other than arthritis medicine. When the symptoms are severe, surgery may be required to realign the kneecap and prevent it from popping out of position. This can be done to prevent further kneecap dislocation.

CHAPTER FIVE

A Lack Of Pyruvate Kinase In The Body

This is a hereditary condition that leads to abnormalities in the red blood cells. Cairns who contract this illness will have anemia, pale gums, a decreased tolerance for exertion, and an enlarged liver and spleen. Sadly, there is no treatment available, and the majority of canines affected by this condition pass away before the age of four. There is a DNA test that can identify the condition in early puppies or in pet parents who are interested in reproducing their animals.

Bleeding Disorders

Dogs can suffer from a wide variety of inherited bleeding problems, including those listed here. They range from being extremely light to being very severe in terms of severity. In many cases, an animal appears to be healthy until it sustains a significant injury or undergoes surgery, after which they may experience considerable bleeding. People living in Cairns have an increased risk of contracting a number of uncommon blood illnesses.

Hemolytic anemia and thrombocytopenia are conditions that manifest themselves in animals whose immune systems have become dysregulated to the point that they begin to attack the animal's own red blood cells or platelets. Your dog will rapidly develop anemia, weakness, and lethargic behavior if the immune system begins to attack red blood cells. Instead of having the typical brilliant pink tone, his gums will have a pale or yellowish appearance. If his immune system attacks his platelets, his blood won't be able to clot normally, and he may experience unusual bleeding or bruising as a result. Before carrying out any surgical procedures, we are going to check for the presence of these issues by carrying out diagnostic testing for blood clotting. Steroids and other immune-suppressing medications will be prescribed in order to reduce or halt the killing of cells caused by the immune system. It is necessary to receive a transfusion of platelets or red blood cells in an emergency situation on occasion.

Cairn Terriers are prone to developing Von Willebrand's disease, which is a condition of the blood clotting process. Before we proceed with the surgery, we will run diagnostic testing to determine the blood clotting time or a DNA blood test that is specific for Von Willebrand's disease or other disorders with comparable symptoms in order to check for this issue.

Allergies

When a person has an allergy to pollen, mold, or dust, they will experience symptoms such as sneezing and itchy eyes. Dogs do not sneeze when they have allergies; rather, their skin becomes itchy. This type of skin allergy is referred to as "atopy," and many people in Cairns have it.

In most cases, the areas most susceptible to infection include the feet, abdomen, folds of the skin, and ears. The onset of symptoms normally occurs between the ages of one and three, and they may become more severe with each passing year. The most typical symptoms include licking and rubbing the face and paws, as well as having frequent ear infections. The good news is that this ailment may be treated in a variety of ways, and there are numerous solutions available.

Liver Problems

There is a higher risk that your young Cairn will suffer from a condition known as portosystemic shunt in comparison to other dogs (PSS). Because a portion of the blood supply that ought to go to the liver instead flows around it, the liver is deprived of the blood flow that is necessary for it to develop and operate appropriately. In the event that your friend has PSS, his liver will be unable to properly eliminate poisons from his bloodstream. Every time he gets anesthesia, we will evaluate his liver function in addition to performing a routine pre-anesthetic panel so that we can make sure that he does not have this condition. In the event that he develops symptoms like slowed growth or seizures, we will test his blood and perhaps perform an ultrasound check of his liver. It's possible that surgery will be required, but in certain instances, we can treat the condition with a specialized diet and some medications.

Beginning in his middle age, your Cairn Terrier is at risk for developing a chronic liver illness known as hepatitis. This disease affects the liver. In most cases, we identify it with blood testing and a biopsy of the liver, and we treat it with medicine and specific dietary regimens. In most cases, symptoms of liver disease won't show up until a significant portion of the organ has already been damaged or eliminated. We are able to recognize this issue at an earlier stage when it is more curable if we conduct routine blood tests and engage in early detection and intervention.

CHAPTER SIX

Cushing's Syndrome Is Also Known As Hyperadrenocorticism

Cushing's disease is characterized by an abnormality of the adrenal glands that results in an excessive amount of steroid hormone production. This is an issue that affects a lot of dogs, and unfortunately, your Cairn is more likely to be impacted than other dogs. In most cases, the ailment progresses quite gradually, making it simple to ignore the warning indications in their early stages. The signs and symptoms of this condition include excessive thirst and urination, an increased appetite, and decreased activity level. In later stages, the condition is characterized by a potbelly, weak skin, and hair loss. The treatment typically consists of oral drugs, and careful collaboration with us is required to ensure that the correct dosage is administered.

Necrosis Of The Hip

It is possible for young Cairn Terriers to develop a painful form of degenerative hip disease known as Legg-Calve-Perthes Disease. It is still not totally understood what causes this ailment, although it is assumed to be an issue with the blood flow to the hip, which causes the femoral head (the top of the thigh bone) to become brittle and readily fracture. The specific etiology of this condition is still not completely understood. Ouch! This condition, which typically manifests itself between the ages of six and nine months, can cause pain and lameness in either or both of the animal's hind legs, and it frequently necessitates surgical intervention.

Coronary Artery Disease

When Cairn Terriers reach their senior years, heart failure is the most common cause of death that they experience. The majority of cases of canine heart disease are brought on by a valve that has become weak. One of the heart's valves steadily deteriorates to the point where it can no longer close completely.

The subsequent backflow of blood around this valve causes the heart to work harder than it should.

A heart murmur is present in animals that suffer from heart valve disease, which is also referred to as mitral valve disease. We will undertake tests to establish the degree of the condition in your dog if he or she has a heart murmur or other outward indicators suggesting that there may be a problem with the heart. In order to keep an eye on the issue, the previous tests will need to be redone at least once per year.

If the condition of his heart valves is caught in its early stages, we may be able to treat him with medications that will add many years to his life expectancy.

Dental care from a veterinarian, as well as the replenishment of fatty acids, can help prevent heart disease, and maintaining a healthy weight can help reduce the severity of its symptoms.

Bladder Or Kidney Stones

There are several distinct kinds of stones that can develop in either the kidney or the bladder, and Cairn Terriers are more likely than other breeds to experience this condition than any other type of dog. We will periodically analyze his urine to look for telltale indicators that indicate the existence of painful kidney and bladder stones; these stones can cause a lot of discomfort. Urgent medical attention is required if your friend is unable to urinate, has blood in his urine, or is in pain while trying to urinate. Make contact with us right away!

Dysplasia Of The Hip And Elbow

Dysplasia is an inherited disease that can affect the hips as well as the elbows. This condition causes the joints to develop abnormally, which ultimately leads to arthritis. It is possible that your Cairn will experience issues with stiffness in his elbows or hips, particularly as he gets older. If you pay attention, you might observe that he has trouble getting up from lying down or that his legs start to exhibit signs of lameness. We are able to treat the arthritis, and the sooner treatment begins, the better it will be for reducing arthritis-related discomfort and pain. We will take X-rays of your dog's skeleton in order to discover any potential problems in their early stages. In severe and potentially life-threatening conditions, surgery can be a viable treatment choice at times. Keep in mind that overweight dogs are more likely to develop arthritis several years earlier than dogs of normal weight, creating unnecessary pain and suffering for the dog.

Disorders Of The Kidneys

Glomerulonephropathy is an inherited condition that steadily affects your Cairn Terrier's kidneys, causing them to fail, frequently at a young age. The disease is passed down from generation to generation.

Because diseased kidneys release protein into the bloodstream, we may be able to diagnose this condition by analyzing his urine for an abnormally high concentration of protein. We recommend having your pet's urine tested once a year because early detection results in a healthier, happier pet as well as a treatment plan that is simpler and more cost-effective.

CHAPTER SEVEN

How To Take Care Of Your Cairn Terrier When You're Not At Home

The majority of what you can do to ensure the happiness and wellbeing of your dog can be summed up in a single word: common sense. Keep an eye on her diet, make sure she gets plenty of exercise, brush her teeth and coat on a regular basis, and contact us or a pet emergency hospital if something appears out of the ordinary (for a list of things to look out for, see "What to Watch For" below). Be sure to stick to the schedule of checkups and vaccines that we have outlined for her. It is in her best interest. When this time comes, we will do the obligatory "check-ups" on her and perform diagnostic testing for diseases and ailments that are prevalent in Cairns. Signing up for pet health insurance is another extremely crucial step in providing proper care for your animal companion. There is a good chance that she will require various medical tests and operations throughout the course of her life, and having pet health insurance will assist you in meeting the financial obligations associated with these needs.

Care Routines, Diet, And Physical Activity

You can help your Cairn live a longer, healthier, and happier life by incorporating her routine care into your calendar. This will aid her during her entire life. It is impossible to place enough emphasis on maintaining a healthy diet and regular exercise routine.

• Take the same precautions with your pet that you would with a young child. Maintain a closed door policy, be sure to pick up after yourself, and section off rooms as required. She won't be able to get into mischief and she won't be able to access things that she shouldn't put in her mouth because of this.

• Her requirements for personal hygiene are minimal. To avoid getting mats in her hair, brush it as often as necessary and at least once a week. Cairn Terriers typically have healthy teeth, which may be maintained in excellent condition by brushing them at least once every other day.

Even when she was a puppy, you should clean her ears once a week.

Don't be concerned; we'll walk you through it!

• Because she is an intelligent dog with a lot of energy, it is important to keep both her mind and body active; otherwise, she will become bored. After then, nasty things will begin to happen.

• Due to the fact that she has a strong instinct to hunt, she must always be walked on a leash, and the yard must always be fenced in.

As long as she gets regular exercise in the form of walks, she should be fine living in an apartment.

- Maintain a set diet for your dog, and under no circumstances should you feed her table scraps.

- Ensure that she consumes a food of high nutritional value that is suitable for her age.

- Make sure your dog gets enough of exercise on a regular basis, but don't push him too hard at first.

What To Keep An Eye Out For

Any odd symptom could be an indication of a dangerous disease, or it could just be a minor or temporary problem. This is because any abnormal symptom could be a sign of any disease. It is essential to have the ability to determine when it is necessary to seek veterinarian assistance and the degree of urgency involved. There are a number of diseases that can affect dogs, and each of these diseases can generate a distinct mix of symptoms. These symptoms, when taken together, might be an obvious warning that your Cairn Terrier needs assistance.

THE END

Printed in Great Britain
by Amazon